IMAGES
of America

NEW JERSEY'S PALISADES INTERSTATE PARK

This photograph, probably taken around 1910, captures the rugged beauty of the Palisades. The photographer may well have walked out onto a frozen Hudson River to set up his tripod and camera to capture this image of Bombay Hook in Alpine, including the Man-in-the-Rock pillar that juts out from the cliff face.

On the cover: Please see page 28. (Courtesy of the Palisades Interstate Park Commission.)

IMAGES
of America

NEW JERSEY'S PALISADES
INTERSTATE PARK

E. Emory Davis and Eric Nelsen

ARCADIA
PUBLISHING

Published by Arcadia Publishing
Charleston SC, Chicago IL, Portsmouth NH, San Francisco CA

Printed in the United States of America

Library of Congress Catalog Card Number: 2006936425

For all general information contact Arcadia Publishing at:
Telephone 843-853-2070
Fax 843-853-0044
E-mail sales@arcadiapublishing.com
For customer service and orders:
Toll-Free 1-888-313-2665

Visit us on the Internet at www.arcadiapublishing.com

This book is dedicated to the photographers who over the generations
have left so many stirring images of the Palisades—and who far too often
remain anonymous.

CONTENTS

ACKNOWLEDGMENTS

We need first to thank James Hall, the park's superintendent, and Chris Szeglin, assistant superintendent, for their unflagging support not just of this project but of all our efforts to preserve—and tell—the story of the Palisades and this park.

Our colleague and friend Anthony G. Taranto Jr. lent us his keen photographer's eye, which proved invaluable in selecting and arranging the images in these pages. (Several of Tony's own photographs appear here, in chapters 1 and 7.)

Erin Stone, our editor at Arcadia, was a delight to work with from start to finish.

This book would not have been possible without the efforts of a dedicated group of volunteers and staff who have spent hundreds of hours identifying, sorting, scanning, and cataloging over 3,000 images to date: Christina Fehre, Connie Ftera, Chad Hill, Ron Keeney, Gayle Metzkier, Carol and Gene Pantuck, Veronica Sison, and Mindy Smith. It was Paul Merino who first set us down this road and Jay Wolf who has kept us on it.

Then there are the extraordinary individuals, literally spread across the Atlantic seaboard, who have donated images or insight—or both: Barrie Tait Collins (Bethany, Connecticut); Suzanne Conklin (Suffern, New York); Margaret Dean (Venice, Florida); Joseph Ellicott (right here in Alpine); Carole K. Harris (Brooklyn); Brian McGowan (New Orleans); Marion Ordway (Savannah, Georgia); Mercedes Alvarez Rionda (Manhattan); Helen Soka (Paramus, New Jersey); John Spring (Cresskill, New Jersey); Susan Sundermeyer (Sandwich, Massachusetts); and Edna and Robert Wilson (also in Alpine). Each of these individuals has enriched not only this book but our lives as well. (We are saddened to note three who are no longer with us: Peggy, Joe, Bob—we miss you.)

Finally we need to thank our families and friends—in particular John and Melinda Davis and Anthony O'Donnell, and Milt Nelsen and Carol Hoernlein—without whose encouragement, support, and forbearance this work could not have been completed.

INTRODUCTION

When the work of acquiring the land was done, the Commission had as raw material thirteen and a half miles of cliffs and talus slope and shore front, badly scarred in some places, but on the whole retaining so much of their original wild and inaccessible character that a writer of that time called them "the Unknown Palisades."

The Palisades Interstate Park: A History of Its Origin and Development
The Commissioners of the Palisades Interstate Park, 1929

For many who live in the New York metropolitan area, the rugged land that comprises the New Jersey Section of the Palisades Interstate Park remains "the Unknown Palisades." It is hard to think of another well-known landmark—seen by many thousands daily from the George Washington Bridge alone—that is so relatively unexplored. Beyond the park's well-used riverfront picnic areas, out along its 30 miles of hiking trails, it is not uncommon for hikers to find an hour or two of solitude, half a mile across the Hudson River from Manhattan, the Bronx, and Yonkers. Hikers discover hidden glens with cascading brooks—as well as forgotten stone jetties and foundation remains that speak of bygone times. Who built that jetty, and for what purpose? Whose house once stood above this overgrown cellar hole? Those are the types of questions this book seeks to answer, with words but mainly with pictures. Those bygone times and forgotten men and women have left us a rich pictorial and photographic legacy.

To the Native Americans who hunted in their forests and camped and fished in their shadows, the Palisades were We-Awk-En—"Rocks That Look Like Trees." The ancient columns of basaltlike trap rock must have inspired wonder among the crew on Henry Hudson's *Half Moon* in 1609. What lay beyond those towering curtain folds of rock that went on almost unbroken for mile after mile along the river's western bank? The answer was a fertile valley, some of the best farmland in the Northeast. But how were the farmers that later settled there to get their harvest to the New York City markets, 10 miles or more down the river that flowed beneath the tall cliffs? In time, with hard labor, mountain passes were transformed into wagon roads. Docks were built at the foot of the cliffs. Armies and foraging parties on both sides of the American Revolution traveled these roads, leaving a record in hand-drawn maps and journal entries.

Through the 19th century, the Hudson River became in a real sense "America's Main Street," and the rugged roads built in Colonial times gave rise to hamlets where boatmen lived and to fishermen's villages along the Palisades riverfront. The growth of the Industrial Age also saw the advent of mills and factories as well as stone quarries along the shorefront, bringing with them waves of immigrant labor. Picnic groves were established in leafy plateaus beneath the cliffs, where thousands of New York's working class might come for an afternoon's "excursion."

Meanwhile, New York's wealthy discovered the lofty heights above the Hudson, and Gilded Age estates began to take advantage of the views from the cliff top—as well as the view that river travelers would have of the stone palaces they built in this spectacular setting, only an hour or two's journey from the city.

By the 1890s, two forces were on a collision course along the Palisades: the Industrial Age's exploitation of nature—specifically, a handful of large quarries that were turning dynamite against the ancient columns of trap rock—and the emerging sense of the innate romance of nature, perhaps best represented by the famous Hudson River school of painting that had flourished earlier in the century. As the devastation of the quarries grew worse each year, the movement to shut them down and preserve the Palisades grew stronger. In 1900, the efforts of a number of dedicated groups and individuals were rewarded with the creation of a unique interstate park, which began to acquire land along the Palisades and to develop beaches, marinas, campgrounds, and other recreational facilities within that land. The new park was 12 miles long in New Jersey, spanning four towns in northeastern Bergen County.

The park revealed its true value, however, during the Great Depression that began in 1929. Strapped with economic hard times, millions chose to come to the new park to enjoy a day's respite from the crisis. Park photographers snapped away. But looming in the background was the brand-new George Washington Bridge—park photographers had captured shots of its construction too—and in time, the gray steel structure would change the park. Sensing the effect the bridge would have on real estate development, the park commission began to acquire cliff-top property as well, bringing to an end the opulent days of cliff-top manor homes and gardens. At the same time, the park became a workplace for hundreds of men and boys employed by the Roosevelt administration's New Deal agencies, creating in stone a legacy that endures to this day.

The last of the park's swimming beaches closed after the 1943 season ("river pollution caused by war conditions" was the reason cited). The park nevertheless has remained an oasis of nature and scenic beauty in an increasingly busy world, an oasis with a rich story to tell.

One

ROCKS THAT
LOOK LIKE TREES

Around Christmastime 1910, New Yorkers were beset by a case of dinosaur fever. The *New York Times* kicked things off on December 21 of that year with a front-page article that began, "The well-preserved skeleton of what appears to have been a dinosaur, 30 to 40 feet long and 15 to 18 feet in height, has been found in the Palisades opposite West 155th Street." The bones had been discovered some months earlier by a group of Columbia University students out "geologizing" along the western banks of the Hudson River, collecting rock specimens from beneath the Palisades. At the time, the fossil—now known to be the remains of a crocodile-like animal called a phytosaur—was thought to be around 10 million years old. Today scientists place its age closer to 200 million years, to around the time that the molten magma that would become the rock that forms the Palisades first "intruded" into the soft sandstones and shales in the area, a volcanic event that occurred underground. Over the course of thousands of years, this magma cooled into diabase rock, and millions of years of erosion eventually revealed the miles of stone columns that the Lenape Indians called We-Awk-En: "Rocks That Look Like Trees."

The Lenape hunted and fished along We-Awk-En for centuries, but the cliffs were a formidable barrier for the Europeans who began to colonize the area in the 17th century. The Palisades impeded their early settlement of the fertile valley beyond the cliffs, forcing the settlers to enter that valley from the smaller rivers that ran through it, such as the Hackensack. In time, however, mountain passes, once trails used by the Lenape, became the routes for primitive farm roads. The landings at their bases teemed with wagons during the fall harvest, the farmers loading their goods onto wooden sloops to be shipped to New York's markets. These same landings and roads were used, in turn, by the armies of the American Revolution, in both skirmishes and larger movements, as the once tranquil setting became ensnared in the passions of global events.

This diagram of the geology of the Palisades was made for the park in July 1940 by geologist M. C. Reichenbecher and naturalist G. W. Higgins. It shows a cross-section of the cliffs at Point Lookout in Alpine, the highest point on the Palisades in New Jersey, with an elevation of 532 feet above sea level. It can be seen that the cliffs are in fact the exposed edge of the cooled diabase sill that extends back to the west (left) from the river. The sill stretches for more than 40 miles along the western shore of the Hudson River, from Staten Island to Rockland County, New York, where it achieves its highest elevation at High Tor Mountain, 827 feet above sea level. More than half a century after it was drawn, the information displayed in the diagram is still considered accurate.

At all times of year, the Palisades offer breathtaking scenery, as shown in this photograph taken at Point Lookout. Note the distinctive columns in the cliff face. (The name Palisades is from the cliffs' resemblance to a palisade, or stockade-type fence.) As the cliffs erode, an entire column will often fall at once, creating a pile of boulders at the base of the cliffs, called talus. The rich soil of the talus slope supports the growth of mature forests beneath the cliffs.

THE DINOSAUR : "OH, DEAR ME, HOW NEW YORK HAS GROWN!"

This cartoon from the *New York Times* ran on Christmas Day 1910, depicting a dinosaur marveling at "how New York has grown." The fossil found along the Palisades that year created a great deal of excitement in the New York metropolitan area. Prior to its discovery, dinosaurs and their fossils had been associated with more far-flung regions, such as the Gobi Desert or the American Southwest. Scientists at the time named it a species of "iguanodon," although modern scientists have determined that it was a phytosaur. The fossil—which is the phytosaur's hindquarters—is still on display in the American Museum of Natural History in Manhattan.

This illustration is the cover of Robert L. Dickinson's *Palisades Interstate Park*, a beautifully hand-illustrated booklet he produced for the American Geographical Society of New York in 1921. The cover depicts a stylized rendering of Henry Hudson's *Half Moon* sailing before the tall cliffs in 1609. Hudson's voyage up the river that would one day bear his name has remained a key image in the romantic traditions associated with the river valley. For the thriving native societies in that valley, however, the sight of the *Half Moon*'s tall white sails marked the beginning of the end of a way of life that had flourished for generations. Barely a decade after Hudson's journey, Europeans were building settlements in the river valley. Most of the newcomers were of Dutch origin. Even after the English took over New Netherland in 1664, much of the Hudson River valley, including the settlements beginning to emerge along the Palisades, remained culturally and linguistically Dutch through the time of the Revolution and into the early 19th century. (Courtesy of the American Geographical Society.)

This Lenape grinding stone was found near Alpine Boat Basin, a reminder of the "Original People" (what *Lenape* means) who inhabited the area. Although they did not establish permanent settlements along the Palisades—the rocky soil beneath the cliffs was not suited to their agricultural practices, and a settlement there would be vulnerable to attack by other tribes—the Lenape nevertheless maintained seasonal encampments along the riverfront to hunt, fish, and trade.

Along the 12-mile length of the park are numerous stone jetties like this one at Huyler's Landing—remnants of some of the earliest European settlements along the river. Not only did these landings facilitate the agricultural settlement of the valley behind the Palisades by providing easier access for shipment of goods, but in time, they also gave rise to hamlets and small villages along the riverfront.

This painting, entitled *The landing of the British forces in the Jerseys on the 20th of November 1776 under the command of the Rt. Honl. Lieut. Genl. Earl Cornwallis*, was painted by Thomas Davies, a British soldier, in that same year. The painting depicts British troops, led by Gen. Charles Cornwallis, arriving at the New Dock (later Huyler's Landing) and their ascent up the Palisades as they make their way to attack American forces under the command of Gen. George Washington at Fort Lee—an attack that the British hoped would serve as a deathblow to the floundering American revolt. Washington got word of the surprise attack the morning of the overnight crossing, as the British approached Fort Lee, and led the American troops on what is now known as the Retreat to Victory. While this was the most significant military action to take place along the Palisades, the area saw a number of smaller skirmishes and conflicts throughout the war. (Image courtesy of the Emmet Collection, Miriam and Ira D. Wallach Division of Art, Prints and Photographs, the New York Public Library, Astor, Lenox and Tilden Foundations.)

Two

ALONG AMERICA'S
MAIN STREET

On a spring evening in 1896, at the riverfront hamlet beneath the Palisades then known as Alpine Landing, it suddenly seemed like the end of the world. Tons of rock thundered down from the steep slope above the landing, some of the stones careening into the houses there. After the dust cleared, one boulder—weighing perhaps 20 tons—stood out in particular, and someone carved into it, "Stone Fell 18 of April 1896." The rock sits there still at what is now called Alpine Boat Basin, serving as a testament to some of the hardships of life beneath the Palisades. Despite these hardships, several hundred men, women, and children chose to live in places like Alpine Landing (originally called Closter Landing) during the 19th century—an indication of the importance of the Hudson River in that time. Many of the men worked as boatmen on the river, first on sailing vessels, later on steamboats. Others were fishermen or dockworkers. There were even a handful of intrepid farmers of the talus slope. As the settlements at the landings grew, tradesmen and merchants found their way to them as well. By midcentury, a boom occurred along the Palisades, as the rock of the talus slope was quarried for use in building the deepwater docks for New York Harbor. The bustling quarries needed labor, and soon immigrants from many nations began to live alongside the mostly Dutch families who had been there for generations. Mills and "bone factories" began to appear along the shorefront, while some Palisades families began to rent their property as "excursion groves."

While no houses were destroyed in the 1896 rock slide, in many ways it foretold of a world about to end. Within a decade, the new Palisades Interstate Park Commission would own most of the land along the Palisades. One by one the signs of these settlements would be torn down—except for one house, still standing next to the 20-ton boulder that might have destroyed it.

The date of this portrait (top left) of Rachel Kearney—and thus her age in the photograph—is unknown. Rachel, born in 1780, lived at Closter (later Alpine) Landing from 1817 until her death in 1870 at the age of 90. When she died, all nine of her children were still alive, and she had at least 50 grandchildren, some of whom still lived in the Alpine Landing area. Most of Rachel's sons followed in their father's footsteps and pursued work on the river, including Gilbert, who became a steamboat master and whose 1874 membership certificate in the Albany Boatmen's Relief Association is shown below. Gilbert's son Monte (top right) was still in Alpine for the 1930 census, his occupation listed as sloop captain. (Above right and below, courtesy of Suzanne Conklin.)

This *c.* 1897 photograph shows the last surviving riverfront house of the Palisades, today known as the Kearney House. Probably built in the 1760s, the Kearney House was one of a cluster of homes along the Hudson River below the Palisades at Alpine Landing in the 19th century and is named for the Kearney family, who lived in the house for most of the 1800s. Rachel Kearney was a widow with three children when she moved into the house with her second husband, James Kearney, in 1817. She raised a total of nine children in the house when it was still only two rooms and an attic. After James's death in 1831, Rachel, still with several young children, began to run a tavern from her home. In roughly 1840, the family built an addition onto the northern side of the house, most likely to accommodate the tavern business, making it the size shown in this photograph. (The large boulder from the previous year's rock slide is also visible, to the left of the houses.)

Above, the Kearney House stands in the center of this view of Alpine Landing from across the Hudson River, taken around 1897. Originally known as Closter Landing, the landing became an important port during the 1800s. From its docks, farmers shipped their goods to New York markets, and the landing was home to many boatmen, laborers, fishermen, and their families. The large complex on the right was a cereal mill, built around 1860. The photograph below, also from around 1897, shows the view looking north from the landing, with the cereal mill on the left. The mill, owned by Col. Sweeting Miles, was steam powered and became one of the largest businesses in eastern Bergen County. It was torn down after being acquired by the park in 1908, its remains probably used as landfill in the park.

Also around 1860, a New Yorker named John Johnson built a "bone factory" about a mile north of Alpine Landing, shown above. Bone factories reflected a reality of life in a horse-powered world: as a matter of course, dead horses needed to be disposed of. At the factory, their bones were ground into bonemeal, which was sold as fertilizer. Below, in around 1897, the view north from Alpine Landing, looking toward Johnson's factory, brings home another truth about bone factories: they were typically sited in remote locations, such as barren stretches along the Palisades, as few people other than the workers employed in them would live near such facilities. Farther north were other bone factories as well as a "gut factory" where entrails were rendered for soap and other products. All of these facilities were isolated from the riverfront hamlets.

In around 1897, an unidentified man, seemingly a laborer, stands with an excellent view of the talus slope behind him. Much of the slope was considered worthless at the start of the 19th century yet ended up making its owners wealthy with the midcentury dock-building boom. The talus quarries employed hundreds of men, many of them new immigrants willing to perform the grueling tasks of breaking and loading stone.

In this undated photograph, Catherine Brown stands before the house she shared with her siblings at Huyler's Landing, named for the prominent Huyler family that owned the land there—as they had once probably owned the Brown siblings' family as slaves. Slavery had been common in Bergen County, and following their emancipation, many former slaves and their descendents found their way to the riverfronts, where work was almost always available. (Courtesy of John Spring.)

Cape Fly Away, north of Alpine Landing, where the house in the photograph above stood, was the site of a farm that had been painstakingly built into the slope above the shore (hundreds of yards of stone terraces still survive in the forest). By the time this photograph was taken—around the beginning of the 20th century—the farm had been abandoned. The cape had become a hamlet where fishermen lived, like the eel fishermen in the photograph below, taken around 1910. The last residents of Cape Fly Away left around the end of the 1920s. The Campbells, the Jordans, the Anthonys, and the Westervelts were among the families at the cape. (Courtesy of Robert Wilson.)

Fishermen's Village, near present-day Englewood Boat Basin, is shown in the undated photograph above. As with most of the riverfront settlements, a geological gap in the cliffs permitted a farm road to be built to the river in Colonial days. (Locally Fishermen's Village was also known as "Pickle Town," after a sloop carrying pickles capsized nearby and its cargo washed ashore there.) Among the families to settle near Fishermen's Village were the Allisons, the Van Wagoners, the Bloomers, and the Crums. Left, Ann Crum, widow of Andrew Jackson Crum and one of the last residents of Fishermen's Village, sits on her porch in the early 20th century. A newspaper story about her at around this time reported that she had never been to New York City, that she thought eating city bread made people sickly, and that she did not believe in elephants.

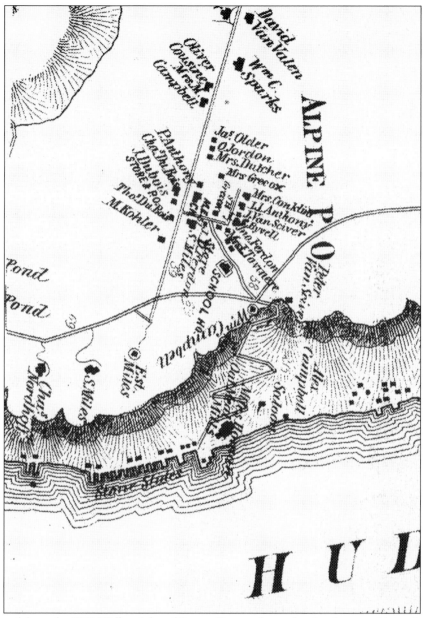

This detail from the 1876 *Walker Atlas of Bergen County* shows the riverfront at Alpine Landing. The Closter Dock Road zigzags down the mountainside to the river at about center. Beneath the main dock at its base are a series of smaller docks labeled "Stone Slides"—these are talus quarries, long wooden ramps built into the hillside and out to deep water; the ramps would be extended upward as the quarrymen worked deeper into the talus slope. There are a school, a feed store, and a store with a post office in the village area at the top of the mountain. Rachel Kearney had died in 1870; her tavern was now gone. (Her daughter Ellen Conklin, who had lived with her at the tavern, had moved after her mother's death to the summit; her house, marked "Mrs. Conklin," is directly alongside the large *P.*) There is a saloon shown now along the Closter Dock Road, above the big Oat Meal Mills. The cluster of houses along the shore at the right side of the map is Cape Fly Away.

23

Excursion trips, offered by companies like N. S. Briggs, became popular during the late 19th century. On these trips, city dwellers would travel by steamboat or special barges to spend a day in the country. Often several thousand people, typically members of a social or ethnic society, would come on these excursions to groves along the Hudson River, Long Island Sound, or the Jersey Shore. Several groves operated at the foot of the Palisades, including Excelsior, Alpine, and Occidental, listed on the back of this postcard advertisement for Briggs. The groves featured playing fields for baseball games and the like, swings, dancing pavilions, kitchens, and bars for the excursionists.

Three

THE GILDED EDGE

Beginning around the time of the Civil War, the summit of the Palisades was "discovered" by those seeking a unique country retreat within easy traveling distance of New York City. Before then, the land at the summit had for the most part been used only as woodlots, with natural gorges in the cliff face turned into "pitching places," where felled timber could be slid down to the shoreline to be shipped to the city as building material or firewood. The cliff top's rocky surface and thin soils—and the need to dig and drill oftentimes several hundred feet through the dense bedrock to create a well—had discouraged settlement there.

As railroad and steamboat lines began to make Bergen County accessible to those who worked in the city, however, the cliff top, with its unique contours and sweeping vistas, began to prove irresistible to some, who set out to build both summer and year-round homes there. Among the first to come were the Lambs, noted stained glass artists; Charles Nordhoff, a newspaper editor (and whose wife, it is thought, first proposed the name Alpine for that part of the Palisades); J. Cleveland Cady, the architect of the first Metropolitan Opera House; and Calvert Vaux, one of the designers of Central Park. Over the next generation or two, many other notables followed.

Some of their estates, such as Manuel Rionda's Rio Vista, grew to epic proportions. (Rio Vista included miles of bridle paths, some of which spanned graceful arched bridges, and several man-made ponds, one of which he opened for local children to swim in.) The estates often included dairy barns and greenhouses that allowed for at least some degree of self-reliance in their lofty isolation.

The days of the cliff-edge estates, however, would prove fleeting. Changing economic fortunes and the development of the modern suburbs—spurred along by a new steel bridge—would ultimately spell their demise.

A *c.* 1871 architect's drawing shows the Palisades Mountain House, a hotel located atop the Palisades in Englewood during the late 19th century. Shown below is an advertisement for the hotel that ran in the *New York Times* on June 28, 1872. One of the finest resorts along the Hudson River, the five-story structure was eventually expanded with two additional wings, making it 600 feet long. It could accommodate up to 500 guests, offering them a wide range of amenities, including a telegraph office, a billiard hall, a bowling alley, a barbershop, a cigar stand, reading rooms, public and private parlors, and reception rooms. Just before opening for its 12th season, the Palisades Mountain House burned to the ground during the night of June 3, 1884. Miraculously none of the roughly 40 people in the hotel at the time—mostly servants—were killed in the fire. (Above, courtesy of Edwin Rizer.)

SUMMER RESORTS.

PALISADES MOUNTAIN HOUSE, ELEVEN MILES FROM THE CITY HALL,

This new and elegant hotel, on the west bank of the Hudson, is now open for the reception of guests. The completeness of its appointments, the salubrity of the air, the grandeur of the views and the facility of communication with the City are unsurpassed by any place in the country. It is under the management of

SYLVANUS T. COZZENS,

HITHERTO THE PROPRIETOR OF COZZENS' WEST-POINT HOTEL.

Communication from New-York by steamers *Adelphi* and *Alexis* at 4 and 5 P. M., foot of Harrison-st.; by Yonkers trains to Inwood, connecting with ferry; or by the Northern Railroad of New-Jersey through Englewood, connecting with stages. For terms apply to the undersigned at the hotel, or by letter to Englewood, N. J.

CHARLES E. MURRAY.

A man drinks from a well on the grounds of Falcon Lodge, the summer home of the Joseph Lamb family in Alpine, around 1900. The Lambs, noted stained glass artists, were probably the first of a number of families to build a home atop the cliffs during the 19th century. Founded in New York City in 1857, J. and R. Lamb Studios remains among the top stained-glass studios in the United States. Many churches in the Palisades area—and across the nation—have Lamb stained glass in them to this day. The photograph below, also taken around 1900, shows the Lamb family's house. The man in the center of the photograph is Joseph Lamb.

In this photograph, probably taken in the early 1900s, a man and a woman, likely members of the Lamb family, rest with their two dogs during an outing by Indian Point along the Palisades in Alpine. The photograph is one of about 30 of Falcon Lodge and the Palisades that Charles Rollinson Lamb, son of Joseph and successor to managing J. and R. Lamb Studios, donated to the park commission shortly before his death in 1942.

The Joseph Lamb family (with some of their dogs) poses for a *c.* 1886 portrait at Falcon Lodge. From left to right are Agnes, Charles, Frederick, Eliza, Richard, Joseph, and Osborn. All the Lambs held a special fondness for the Palisades, and Frederick would be influential in the early efforts to preserve the Palisades. (This copyrighted image used with the permission of Barrie Tait Collins and the Lamb family.)

Falcon Lodge For Sale

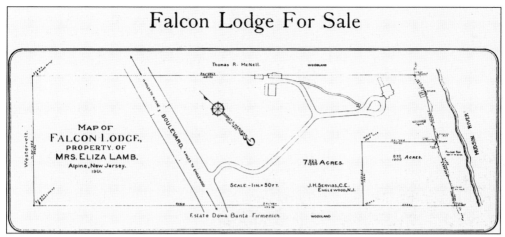

This map of Falcon Lodge, drawn in 1901 when it was put up for sale, shows the layout of the almost eight-acre property. (Courtesy of Barrie Tait Collins.)

Manuel Rionda and his wife, Harriet Clarke Rionda, pose for a photograph on the grounds of their Alpine estate, Rio Vista, around 1920. As is clear from this picture, the Riondas were a close and loving couple. Originally from Noreña, Spain, Manuel Rionda was known as the "Sugar Baron" and owned sugar cane plantations in Cuba. (Courtesy of Mercedes Alvarez Rionda.)

This *c.* 1920 photograph shows the drive leading to the water tower and office at Rio Vista. Manuel Rionda's Alpine estate was the largest on the Palisades, comprising well over 100 acres, and included a pond that Rionda donated for use as a public swimming spot. The tower still stands in the Alpine-Cresskill neighborhood located where his estate once was, a neighborhood that is still called Rio Vista. (Courtesy of Mercedes Alvarez Rionda.)

Manuel Enrique Rionda, a nephew of Manuel Rionda, goes out for a drive on his own Alpine estate, Glen Goin, with his wife, Ellen Goin Rionda (center), and an unidentified woman, around 1920. (Courtesy of Mercedes Alvarez Rionda.)

Harriet Clarke Rionda poses for a portrait around 1920. The Riondas had no children of their own but were part of a large closely knit family (Manuel was one of nine children), and they had a particular affection for their nephew Manuel Enrique, whose mother died in childbirth. Below is a photograph of members of the Rionda family at Rio Vista that was also taken around 1920. From left to right are (first row) Salvador Rionda, another of Manuel's nephews; and Manuel Enrique; (second row) Jose Bernardo Rionda, also Manuel's nephew; Ramona Rionda Alonso, Concha Rionda Jorcano, and Isidora Rionda Noriega, Manuel's sisters; Esperanza Rionda Crowley, Manuel's niece; Manuel; Elena Rionda Doty, another niece; and Leandro Rionda, another nephew. Salvador, Jose Bernardo, Elena, and Leandro were siblings, the children of Manuel's brother Francisco. (Courtesy of Mercedes Alvarez Rionda.)

Ellen Goin Rionda is shown here with a friend on the grounds of Glen Goin around 1920. (Courtesy of Mercedes Alvarez Rionda.)

The wives of some of the men of the Rionda family pose for a photograph at Rio Vista, around 1920. From left to right are Frances Jordan Rionda, Leandro's wife; Mercedes "Cheche" Perez Chaumont Rionda, Jose Bernardo's wife; Ellen Goin Rionda; Harriet Clarke Rionda; and Elena de la Torriente Rionda, wife of Manuel's brother Francisco. Behind the women is the manor house. Also visible is a wrought-iron fence that runs along the edge of cliffs; this fence still stands at Alpine Lookout. (Courtesy of Mercedes Alvarez Rionda.)

The stone columns shown in the photograph above remain standing beside U.S. Route 9W in Alpine. They marked the entrance to Gray Crag, the estate of John and Mable Ringling in the 1920s. Ringling, one of the Ringling brothers of circus fame, bought two existing Palisades estates and combined them into one larger estate. The Ringlings' manor house is shown below, around 1920. The Ringlings later moved to Sarasota, Florida, where the lavish manor house they built there is open to the public as part of the Ringling Museum. (Courtesy of Carole K. Harris.)

Wilma Lois Roberts (on the left) stands with Dulcy Schueler and her children, Bobby and Freddie Schueler, "looking to see what time it is by the sun-dial" on the grounds of Gray Crag in late August 1920. Dulcy Schueler (née Burton) was the sister of Mable Ringling, John Ringling's wife. Below, Roberts stands with Freddie and Bobby on a bridge spanning a gap in the cliffs, just a few yards from the rear of the manor house, which is visible in the background. (That bridge remains although it no longer has the wooden railings and is now just a concrete walkway.) Roberts was a childhood friend of Dulcy Schueler and had traveled by train from her home in Ardmore, Oklahoma, to visit Dulcy and Alma Reid, Dulcy's sister, at the Ringlings' in Alpine. (Courtesy of Carole K. Harris.)

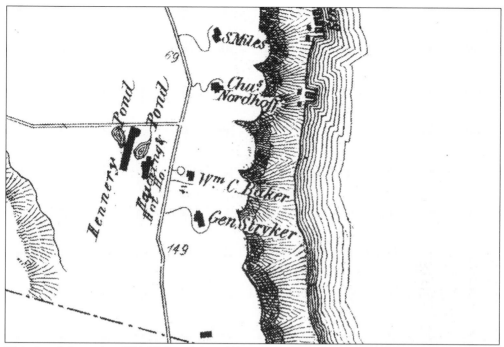

This detail from the 1876 *Walker Atlas of Bergen County*, above, shows part of what became known as Millionaires' Row in Alpine. "S. Miles" shows the estate of Col. Sweeting Miles, who operated the big riverfront mill at Alpine Landing. Charles Nordhoff was a newspaper editor and travel writer whose wife is credited with coining the name *Alpine* for the area. In the illustration from the atlas below, the estate of W. C. Baker (also shown on the map above) is portrayed from a bird's-eye view above the cliffs. Baker operated an innovative steam-heated chicken farm near his estate, which he named Cliff Dale. Note the large hennery shown nearby to his home on the map.

George A. Zabriskie acquired the Cliff Dale estate around 1911. This photograph of the rear of the new manor house he had built was taken around that time and shows the grandeur of the mansion, as well as some of the estate's extensive and elaborate gardens. Cliff Dale was Zabriskie's summer home, with his year-round residence in New York City. Like other estates atop the Palisades, Cliff Dale was razed in the 1930s to make way for the construction of the Palisades Interstate Parkway. The foundation of the manor house remains in the park today, and some of the plants from the gardens that once decorated the grounds continue to grow along the cliff edge.

Zabriskie, shown here in an undated photograph, was a flour merchant. A bachelor and a man of many and eclectic interests—from Revolutionary history to polar exploration to writing *The Bon Vivant's Companion*, a guide to cocktail mixing—Zabriskie also served as president of the New York Historical Society. (Courtesy of Marion Ordway.)

This *c.* 1911 photograph shows the interior of the manor house of Zabriskie's Cliff Dale estate. As can be seen here, the house was lavishly decorated, with an often interesting mix of styles.

This patio, also a part of the Cliff Dale manor house, overlooked a section of the estate's gardens. The gardens that were immediately behind the house are shown in the photograph below. The gardens included man-made ponds, statues, winding paths and stairways, and a number of exotic plants. Note that the cliff edge is just beyond the pond.

The structure above is probably the gatehouse to Cliff Dale, where a groundskeeper or estate superintendent may well have lived. The estate's barn, in the photograph below, is a reminder that many grand estates of the time were at least partly self-sufficient, having their own cows for milk and butter, their own chickens for eggs. Some also grew fresh vegetables on the grounds or even had greenhouses to grow both vegetables and flowers. (Above, courtesy of Marion Ordway.)

The photograph above shows the manor house at Penlyn, one of the last of the Palisades estates, built in the late 1920s for the family of Henry Herbert Oltman, shown at left. Oltman held a seat on the New York Stock Exchange and had summered in Alpine in cottages he owned on the property until he decided to make it his year-round residence. He commuted to Wall Street by having his chauffeur drive him to Jersey City—dropping his daughter Margaret off at the Dwight School in Englewood on the way—and then taking the ferry to the city. (Courtesy of Margaret Dean.)

Among the many handsome rooms at Penlyn was the library shown in the photograph above. Oltman suffered some financial reversals in the late 1930s and was compelled to give Penlyn up for sale (part of the sales brochure for the estate is shown below). He died in 1946. (Courtesy of Margaret Dean.)

1756-B

GROUNDS: Beautiful **9½-acre estate,** between Sylvan Blvd. and the edge of the Palisades, in **Alpine, N. J.** The location is ideal; there is approximately 670 ft. of cliff frontage, with an impressive view of the Hudson River, far below, and the Yonkers shore and skyline. The wooded land on two sides of the property is owned by the state.

A private drive with a low stone wall and cement curbing leads through lovely cleared woodland, over a stone bridge across a pretty little brook, to the nicely set, spacious home. The grounds are fully landscaped, with lawns, formal flower gardens, kitchen garden, terraces, stone walls, shrubs, and trees kept in fine condition by tree surgeons. Everything about this property has been intelligently, artistically planned and carried out with fine materials and the best of workmanship. The result is a pleasantly, quietly beautiful home, pervaded by a comfortable sense of order, convenience and charm. Many excellent country clubs are near, and all kinds of sports facilities. Alpine is 2 miles distant, with a ferry to Yonkers; R. R. station, schools and shopping center in Englewood, 3 miles. N. Y. C., 9 miles, over excellent roads to the George Washington Bridge.

RESIDENCE: Fieldstone, English, of the most modern construction and appointments. Walls of cinder clock and stone, with a heavy slate roof, steel casement windows, copper screens. African wood and teak floors. Brass plumbing, septic tank. Town water. Pyrofax gas. Telephone.

FIRST FLOOR: Large panelled living room. Solarium with fountain. Flower room. Office. Panelled library. Foyer and hall. Powder room and lavatory. Partially panelled dining room with hand painted walls. Butler's pantry. Kitchen. Servants' dining room. Laundry.

SECOND FLOOR: 6 master bedrooms, 1 panelled. 5 baths, with hand painted walls. Large papered closets. Servants' wing: 4 bedrooms, 2 baths.

THIRD FLOOR: Studio room—2 master bedrooms and 1 bath. Trunk room. Cedar closet.

BASEMENT: Boiler room with Bryan heating (vapor vacuum), hot water boiler, Oil burner with 1500 gal. tank—wood room—2 store rooms.

GARAGE UNIT: Stone construction, built 1930. Includes 3-car garage, 2 single rooms and 1 bath. Superintendent's cottage with living room, kitchen, dining alcove, 3 bedrooms, bath, lavatory. Electrical room, brick-insulated pumphouse. Pump operates an Artesian well which cost $10,000. Entire unit heated by vapor steam heat, oil burner.

OTHER BUILDINGS: 1-car garage. Tool house with 2 rooms. Dog kennels. **Main Cottage:** Frame, heated by fireplaces. Living room, dining room, kitchen, screened porch, 4 master bedrooms, 2 baths, lavatory. Servants' unit: 2 rooms and bath, kitchen, pantry, cellar with 1 room and bath, wine and vegetable storage rooms. 2-car garage. **West Cottage:** 2 bedrooms and bath, living room, kitchen and porch. Unheated. Playhouse with 1 room.

Behind Penlyn was an elaborate garden—Henry Herbert Oltman's wife Jessie's passion—that included the fountain shown in the photograph above. A favorite place for young Margaret Oltman was "the point," below, from which she could watch the comings and goings of the Yonkers Ferry and explore the rugged woods and cliffs of the Palisades. (Courtesy of Margaret Dean.)

Four

THE PUSH FOR PRESERVATION

Through most of the 19th century, quarry operations along the Palisades mined the talus slope beneath the cliffs. Long ramplike wooden docks were built out to the deep water offshore. Workers did most of the quarrying by hand, breaking the rock into "handy"-sized pieces (meaning one man could handle them) with sledges and picks and then loading them onto sailing vessels for the trip to New York Harbor, where the rock was used to build the docks of the growing seaport.

Toward the end of the century, this began to change with the demand for gravel for roadbeds and concrete. As the quarries grew, they began to use dynamite to blast down the columns of the cliff face itself; in essence, the quarries were creating their own talus. It was across the river, in New York, where the outcry against these quarries began. A treasured view was being defaced, and by the 1890s, the topic of preventing this "vandalism" became a regular feature of news stories and editorials in the newspapers. Championed by Andrew H. Green and the American Scenic and Historic Preservation Society, the one thing the preservation effort lacked was an ally on the New Jersey side of the river, where the quarrying was actually occurring. That ally finally emerged in the New Jersey State Federation of Women's Clubs, which took on the formidable quarrymen's lobby in Trenton and eventually got the state to sign onto the creation of an interstate commission with New York in 1900. (The governor of New York at the time was Theodore Roosevelt, who would soon after become the president most associated with conservation and parks.)

With the aid of several philanthropic families and individuals, the commission quickly set to work acquiring the Palisades shoreline and cliff face from Fort Lee to the New York state line. They sought not just to preserve the landscape but to transform portions of it into a great "playground," where millions might find recreation and relief from the teeming cities.

Carpenter Brothers' stone quarry in Fort Lee, shown in these two photographs, was the most notorious of the large quarries of the end of the 19th century. At the peak of its operation, Carpenters' was blasting 12,000 cubic yards of rock each day.

The large quarries of the 1890s included ancillary structures like those shown in these photographs, with buildings that housed steam-driven rock-crushing machinery and docks that incorporated conveyer belts to load the crushed stone onto barges.

The devastation caused by the large quarries is clearly shown in this photograph of Carpenters' quarry. Note how the forested talus slope beneath the cliffs is suddenly replaced by piles of

blasted rock where the quarry begins. While Carpenters' was the largest, there were a number of quarries of similar size in operation along the Palisades at the time.

As early as 1894, articles such as that on the left, from the *New York Times*, began to appear, addressing concerns about the quarrymen's work. By 1897, the New Jersey State Federation of Women's Clubs had joined the fight to preserve the Palisades. In the photograph below, during the annual conference of the state federation that year, a group of the women takes an inspection tour of the quarry operations by boat. By 1900, two decades before women's suffrage, the women had succeeded in convincing the states of New York and New Jersey to band together to form an interstate commission to close down the quarries and to acquire the Palisades land for public use. A number of prominent and wealthy families and individuals also contributed to the effort, including J. P. Morgan, who donated the funds needed to close Carpenters'. The quarry ceased operation on Christmas Eve 1900.

During the first decade of the 20th century, the new interstate commission concentrated on acquiring the land along a 12-mile stretch of the Palisades. In 1907, it acquired an 11-acre parcel in Alpine that included the house in this photograph—what would become known as the Kearney House. This photograph was taken in 1908 by Rudolph Eickemeyer Jr., a well-known photographer of his day. (Collection of the Hudson River Museum, Yonkers, New York. Gift of the Estate of Mary Colgate, 37.107.)

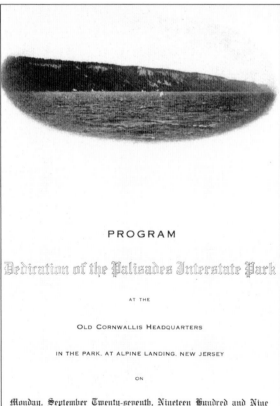

PROGRAM

Dedication of the Palisades Interstate Park

AT THE

OLD CORNWALLIS HEADQUARTERS

IN THE PARK, AT ALPINE LANDING, NEW JERSEY

ON

Monday, September Twenty-seventh, Nineteen Hundred and Nine

AT ELEVEN O'CLOCK IN THE FORENOON

On September 27, 1909, a formal dedication ceremony was held for the new Palisades Interstate Park. The ceremony, which included the governors of both New York and New Jersey among its distinguished guests, was held at what was then called the Old Cornwallis Headquarters (today the Kearney House). At the time, it was believed that Gen. Charles Cornwallis had used the house as his headquarters for a night during the British invasion of New Jersey in 1776. Later research would prove this to be folklore—a myth that resulted in the preservation of the house, now the last of its kind beneath the Palisades in New Jersey. The dedication ceremony was part of a regionwide event called the Hudson-Fulton Celebration, which commemorated the 300th anniversary of Henry Hudson's exploration of the river, and the (approximate) centennial of Robert Fulton's steamboat *Clermont*.

During the first decades of the commission's existence, a tremendous amount of work was done to convert the rugged terrain of the Palisades into a park for public use. Horse-drawn carts and hard manual labor were among the equipment used for this transformation, as shown in the photograph above, in which workers construct a picnic area along the shore. Below, a seawall is constructed in the remote Forest View area at the northern end of the park.

One of the more ambitious projects undertaken by the park during its early years was the construction of a road from the cliff top to the shore in Englewood Cliffs. This road followed the route of an earlier one used by the Palisades Mountain House to bring guests from a steamboat landing at the riverfront to the grand resort at the summit. The modern road, however, would be used by automobiles traveling to and from a new ferry line from Dyckman Street in upper Manhattan. Using the rock cleared away during the construction of this road, the park was able to build a public marina, Englewood Boat Basin, at the base of the cliffs.

The park drew in visitors almost immediately after its creation, even while its facilities were still being built. By 1920, around the time this photograph was taken, more than a million people were using the new park each year. More than half of them came by ferry from Manhattan. Camping was a popular pastime for many park visitors. Camping permits were issued for $1 per week.

Among the many concerns for the new park during its development was to provide its patrons with safe drinking water, and miles of waterlines had to be laid down across the rugged terrain. This was hardly a concern for park visitors themselves, like the woman pictured above, who were able to simply enjoy the scenery and a refreshing drink by the shore.

From its earliest days, the park was a haven for Scout groups, like the Girl Scouts pictured here.

Another draw in the park was its bathing beaches, where visitors could spend a hot summer's day by the shore. Refreshment stands were set up to provide food and beverages to beachgoers.

Park visitors enjoyed canoeing as well as swimming in the waters of the Hudson River. Canoeing was an immensely popular activity during the second decade of the 20th century through the 1930s. It is difficult to find a photograph of the park's waterfront from this time that does not show a canoe.

With over a million visitors a year—coming by ferry, automobile, and canoe—the park needed to hire a police force to maintain order. Part-time officers supplemented the year-round force in the warm weather months. In the somewhat whimsical photograph at right, almost certainly staged, the policeman seems to be admonishing the young women for picking flowers. More serious concerns included keeping a watchful eye on the scores of campfires burning in the park and dealing with occasional thefts or acts of vandalism. Below is the park's 1927 police pistol team, during a pistol match at which it won the F.W. Hopkins Trophy.

With direct access to Manhattan via a pedestrian ferry that ran in the warm weather months from 158th Street, the Hazard's Beach area at the southern end of the park in Fort Lee, shown in these photographs, was among the busiest areas in the early years. The large building in the photograph below was the first of the park's bathhouses, built in 1916. The bathhouse provided changing rooms and lockers, as well as an open-air upstairs picnic area with refreshment stand. Hazard's took its name from the Hazard Powder Company, which had maintained a dock here for dynamite delivery to the nearby quarries.

As the Hazard's area bustled at the southern end of the park, right, at the northern end, an equally busy area was growing, Forest View, shown below, which boasted campgrounds, a picnic pavilion, a ball field, and a boat basin. What both areas had in common was a lack of accommodation for automobiles. Visitors came on foot or, more likely, from the river—by ferry at Hazard's and by excursion boat or personal watercraft at Forest View.

By the peak years of its operation in the late 1920s, the Dyckman Street Ferry, whose New Jersey terminal at Englewood Boat Basin is shown above, was transporting over a million vehicles a year. Along with travelers simply passing through to other destinations, many used the ferry as a means to get to and from the park for a day's outing, such as the people shown in the photograph on the left.

In 1928, the park constructed a new administration building at the summit of the Palisades in Alpine. The building would house the park's administrative and engineering offices, as well as the park police station, until the building's demolition in the 1950s, as the Palisades Interstate Parkway was constructed. The photograph above shows the building during construction; below is the finished structure around 1933.

As the park continued to grow, survey crews were kept busy plotting new roads and other facilities. Above, on February 25, 1931, surveyors are charting the course of the southern portion of Henry Hudson Drive, an ambitious seven-mile roadway begun more than 10 years earlier. In the photograph below, the surveyor is on Hudson Terrace in Fort Lee, in anticipation of a momentous new project that was occurring at the park's very doorstep: a new bridge being built from Fort Lee into Manhattan.

During its construction, the new bridge was called simply the Hudson River Bridge. When it opened to traffic in the fall of 1931, it was christened the George Washington Bridge. The impact of this structure was felt in the park even during its construction (during which park workers took the photographs on this page). The New Jersey tower was built directly in front of Hazard's Beach, and the Port Authority of New York and New Jersey, which oversaw the construction, built a temporary beach and bathhouse just to the north for use during the construction. Hazard's Beach reopened thereafter, but within a matter of years, the pedestrian ferry from 158th Street went out of business due to competition from the bridge, and Hazard's Beach would soon close as well. It was the first of many changes the bridge would bring.

With the new bridge in the background, work progresses on Henry Hudson Drive in this photograph taken around 1932.

Five

THE GREAT PLAYGROUND NEXT DOOR

For a park created literally on the eve of 20th century, the most dynamic period of its first century of existence undoubtedly occurred during the years between the stock market crash of October 1929 and America's entry into World War II in the early 1940s. A great many factors were in play at the park during those years, most prominent among them the Great Depression that enveloped the nation—indeed, much of the world—through the 1930s.

For millions of families, at a time when as many as one in four able-bodied American men was unable to find work, the park represented an inexpensive and convenient escape—if only for an afternoon—from economic hard times. For the price of a ferry ride, families could spend a day picnicking and frolicking in the cool waters of the Hudson River. Attendance at the park soared during the early 1930s, when the crisis was at its worst, and then began a slow decline as the economy started to improve later in the decade, only to jump back up with the start of the war and its attendant travel restrictions.

Another factor in play was the opening of the George Washington Bridge in October 1931. Almost at once, the park began to feel the effects of the new bridge. For example, the ferry lines that operated from the park, and from which the park drew a commission on ticket sales, began to lose revenue. To recoup the loss, the park began to charge admission fees at its beaches for the first time: 10¢ for those over 12.

Another factor was the influx of workers that came with the various agencies of the Roosevelt administration's New Deal programs. The efforts of these agencies in the park will be chronicled in chapter 6. This chapter looks at the park as it was seen through the eyes of the millions who came to it for respite from the worst economic crisis in American history and at the start of a war that engulfed the entire world.

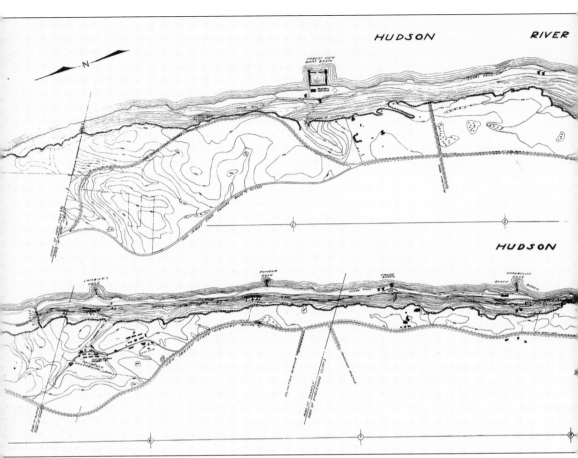

This park map was made in 1936, when the park's facilities were running at full tilt. It divides the 12-mile length of the park into two halves, the northern half on top, the southern half below. Five bathing beaches are shown, including a private one for the "camp colony" at Ross Dock, as well as Canoe Beach, which was a designated canoe landing spot. The Tourist Camp,

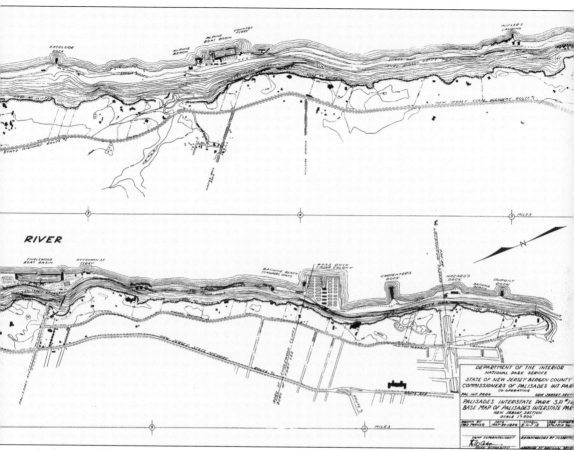

RIVER

which is not labeled, is directly above the Dyckman Street Ferry. Just south of the Forest View Boat Basin is a baseball diamond. Note the many structures shown on top of the cliffs: these are mostly estates, with their manor houses and various outbuildings. Within several years of this map's production, most of these would be torn down (see chapter 6).

Through the 1930s, many visitors continued to arrive by excursion boats, such as the *Warwick*, shown docked at Twombly's Landing on July 22, 1931. (The Twomblys had donated their property to the park with the specific request that it be used as a picnic grove for disadvantaged children.) The park's large Forest View area, below, in a photograph taken on the same day, was accessible almost exclusively by water, and there was no automobile access. It was often rented out by large organized groups of 2,000 or more, most often social or ethnic societies from New York City that came by excursion boat for a weekend afternoon outing. This is likely the case for the African American group shown in the Forest View pavilion in this photograph.

Many visitors also came by automobile, as can be seen in this photograph, also taken around 1931, showing the parking area by Englewood Boat Basin and Bloomer's Beach. The large structure in the background was one of a pair of two-story pavilions that bracketed either end of the boat basin. The cars in the foreground have New Jersey license plates. Other cars in the busy parking area undoubtedly came from New York, via the Dyckman Street Ferry.

In the photograph above, taken around 1932, canoes are pulled up at Carpenter's Beach, just north of the brand-new George Washington Bridge in Fort Lee. In the background is the Ross Dock Camp Colony, which is also shown in the photograph below, taken around the same time, as seen from the cliff top. The park's 1932 *Annual Report* noted that almost 3,000 persons used the facility, which was open from May 15 to October 1 and was "equipped with many conveniences such as city water, hot and cold showers, sanitary sewerage, street layout, trees and shrubs, a rustic cabin housing the resident camp manager and camp store. The entire area, including private bathing beach, is enclosed by strong wire fence, thus excluding the general public." Campers stayed for anywhere from one week to the entire season.

One of the largest bathing beaches in the park was Undercliff Beach in Englewood Cliffs, about half a mile north of the Englewood area, shown in these photographs taken around 1932. The large bathhouse, of similar design to the one at Hazard's Beach, was built in 1922 (its fortlike ruins are still along the Shore Trail). Bathers could walk north from the Englewood area and the Dyckman Street Ferry, or they could take their cars up Henry Hudson Drive and park at a large parking field and picnic area on the tree-lined slope directly above the bathing area. Park lifeguards rescued hundreds of bathers annually, and no lives were lost at the beaches throughout the busy decade of the 1930s (even if the lifeguard "on duty" in the photograph below appears a bit distracted).

Bloomer's Beach, shown in this photograph taken around 1932, was the closest to the Dyckman Street Ferry and thus, although smaller than Undercliff and Hazard's, was one of the busier beaches in the park. The park's *Annual Report* for 1932 estimated that about 130,000 people used the bathhouses at Hazard's and Undercliff Beaches but that "in addition to these, about 210,000 made use of the smaller dressing rooms provided at Bloomer's, Alpine and Quinn's

Beaches. Besides these, there were many persons who did not use the bathhouses, but who came to the Park in bathing suits and removed their outer wraps upon arrival." The dressing rooms can be seen just right of center in this photograph, with a set of stairs leading up to them. A larger stone bathhouse was built at Bloomer's in 1934.

At the Alpine area, in addition to the bathing beach, a wading pool for younger children was built in 1932, shown in this photograph probably taken the same year. In order to get this shot, the photographer would have had to position himself, very noticeably, on the roof of the new children's bathhouse, also built that year (which probably explains why so many people in the shot are looking at the camera).

These photographs also show the Alpine area around 1932. In addition to the new wading pool and children's bathhouse, that year the area's playground was moved next to the bathing beach to enlarge the parking accommodations, and two new drinking fountains were installed, one of which is visible in the photograph below.

One of the Dyckman Street ferryboats can be seen crossing the river in this photograph of Bloomer's Beach taken around 1932, while the smokestacks and pilothouses of another ferry already in the dock can also be made out. In 1932, vehicles using the ferry crossing dropped to around 300,000, from the record highs of over a million in the three previous years. The cause of this decline is visible in the background: the new George Washington Bridge, which opened on October 25, 1931. Also visible in the photograph are the fences that were erected in the river around the beach. The swift river currents could be perilous even for strong swimmers. The fences also kept river debris from drifting into the bathing area.

In one of the big two-story pavilions at either end of Englewood Boat Basin were a downstairs cafeteria and an upstairs beer garden, serving "Beer on Draught." The exterior shot, above, was taken in 1936; the interior, below, while undated, was probably taken around the same time. In addition to a wide selection of sandwiches, items on the menu included fresh tomato juice (10¢), vegetable soup (10¢), hamburger steak (35¢), corn beef and cabbage (50¢), Italian spaghetti and meat sauce (35¢), and spring lamb (50¢). Drake's cakes and Kellogg's cornflakes were also on the shelves, while a sign on the wall informed patrons they had to be 21 years old to purchase alcohol.

In this photograph taken around 1933, a group of canoeists relaxes after a race along the shore of the Hudson River. The crews of the ferries were known to complain of canoeists trying to grab hold for a tow across the river—a decidedly unsafe maneuver. Some recall canoeing out to a barge and asking permission to come aboard, with their canoes, for a unique camping trip on the Hudson.

Taken from the roof of a picnic shelter at the Alpine area on July 14, 1935, this photograph shows the playground beside the beach and the wading pool. Note that all the men have their chests covered, a fashion that was about to change; by the late 1930s, most of the men at the park's beaches would be going "topless."

These photographs were taken at Bloomer's Beach on the same day, July 14, 1935, as the previous photograph. The large stone building in the background, above, is the bathhouse built by the CWA the previous year.

Camp Palisades, also called the Tourist Camp, on top of the cliffs in Englewood Cliffs, shown above around 1932, was billed as the closest campground of its sort to New York City, and it became a popular place for families traveling to the city, as well as for college students on their summer breaks. In particular, many women's colleges sponsored educational travel trips for their students over the summer break, and they would stay at Camp Palisades and travel into the city for lectures and other activities. The photograph below was taken in 1938 at the camp's entrance at the top of Palisade Avenue.

In addition to a pair of motorized refreshment trucks, there were at least a dozen refreshment stands operating in different areas throughout the park. In the interior shot above, taken in 1938, probably at one of the stands at the Alpine area, among the items on the shelves are candy bars and cigarettes, Cracker Jacks and White Owl cigars, and bottles of soda and beer. Below, also in 1938, a gas attendant steps out of the park's newest refreshment stand, State Line Lookout's Lookout Inn. New Deal workers had begun construction on the building, which boasted two large fireplaces, the year before, using native Palisades stone and chestnut logs. The stand is still in operation today (though there are no longer gas pumps available in the parking area, and the building is now enclosed).

These photographs, taken in 1938, show the park's Undercliff Picnic Area, along Henry Hudson Drive, situated directly above Undercliff Beach. Both charcoal grills and open fire pits were available for visitors. The area is rarely opened to cars today but serves as a picnic spot for hikers and cyclists.

Above, park police officers Bill Luthin (left) and Joe Corring stand before the Dyckman Street Ferry terminal at the south end of Englewood Boat Basin in 1938. The ferry service was struggling to stay in business at this point, with the previous year's passage down to just 157,621 vehicles. (Yet it also carried 387,463 pedestrians across the river—most of whom were headed to the park.) Below, also in 1938, cars and passengers disembark from the *F.R. Pierson*, one of the boats operated by the Yonkers Ferry. By this time, even though it operated smaller boats on a more limited schedule, the Yonkers Ferry was taking more vehicles than Dyckman. The reason: it was farther from the new bridge that was hurting the Dyckman Street business.

On July 2, 1939, swimmers enjoy the waters of the Hudson River from a float at the Alpine area, with Bombay Hook—the far point of land that juts into the river—as the backdrop. By this time, only Alpine, Undercliff, and Bloomer's Beaches were being operated. Hazard's had closed several years earlier because of reduced ferry ridership since the opening of the George Washington Bridge. Additionally, the improving economy allowed many to travel to more distant destinations for their recreation, and new facilities, such as Jones Beach on Long Island, were attracting people who had formerly come to the Palisades beaches.

A group of Boy Scouts poses during a camping trip in the park in 1939. Although camping is no longer permitted, many Scouts continue to backpack through the park on their way to a pair of Scout camps that adjoin it in Alpine.

Children play in a sandbox at the Englewood area in this photograph taken on August 1, 1939.

A group of women stops for a picnic along the Shore Trail in 1939. The park created a number of such rustic "picnic tables" in its more remote areas, just large square stones with smaller stones around them for seats. Hikers often encounter these today, especially during the winter months, when there is less foliage to obscure areas off the trails.

On May 30, 1939, a park policeman directs traffic at the intersection of U.S. Route 9W and Alpine Approach Road, the road leading to the Yonkers Ferry (note the sign) and the Alpine Boat Basin, Beach, and Picnic Area. The large building is the park's administration building, built in 1928. This is one of a series of photographs taken that day at this location, part of a traffic-flow study.

Seen from the cliff top, the *John J. Walsh* departs from Alpine for Yonkers. The *Walsh*, only about a year old when this photograph was taken in 1939, was painted silver and had an unusual "futuristic" look. It was designed to be able to go through ice in winter and, like most vehicular ferries, to move forward in either direction, but it was controlled from a single pilothouse amidships (most such ferries have two pilothouses, one at either end). Although its ridership declined somewhat due to competition from the George Washington Bridge, the Yonkers Ferry service was able to stay in operation until 1957, when a drastic decrease in business was caused by the opening of another bridge—the Tappan Zee—and it was finally forced to close. The park then expanded the boat basin into the area of the former ferry slip.

By 1937, 30 rustic three-room cabins had been built, all with fireplaces, at the Ross Dock Camp Colony. Campers, like those shown in this photograph taken on August 6, 1939, could rent the cabins on a weekly basis during the season, which lasted from April through December. Some men commuted to work in the city by ferry and rejoined their families at the camp in the evening.

Fishing and crabbing in the Hudson River were popular activities in the park and remain so to this day (although restrictions have been placed on what is considered safe to eat, and shad remain the only fish that can be commercially harvested from the river). This photograph, taken on August 1, 1939, shows men crabbing from a pier at the Englewood Boat Basin.

Park visitors enjoy the view from Point Lookout, the cliff's highest point in the park, at State Line Lookout in 1939. The road that passed just along the cliff edge was the northbound U.S. Route 9W, which was redirected farther west after the construction of the Palisades Interstate Parkway.

This photograph, taken from the George Washington Bridge in 1940, shows Ben Marden's Riviera nightclub, in Fort Lee, perched atop the Palisades above the park. The art deco–style nightclub, which billed itself as "America's Showplace" and which saw some of the most famous acts of the day perform on its revolving stage, opened shortly after the bridge did. For the park, it was a sign of what might befall the rest of the cliff top.

In 1940, the park continued to operate Bloomer's Beach, above, and Alpine Beach, below. Although records indicate that both suffered a decline in visitors, they obviously remained popular with many people in the summer.

These two photographs were taken at Alpine, the picture above in 1940 and the one below on July 26, 1941. By this time, the style of bathing suits has changed, and almost all men are wearing only trunks. By 1941, Undercliff Beach had closed, leaving only Alpine and Bloomer's Beaches open.

In 1940, a lifesaving demonstration was conducted at Bloomer's Beach. Chief lifeguard George Dunovan performs the demonstration, using the most advanced lifesaving techniques of the day. (The modern lifesaving method of CPR had not yet been developed.) The park also filmed the demonstration, and the cameraman is visible in the top photograph.

In order to keep the park accessible to visitors, then as now, occasional rock slides needed to be quickly cleared from park roads, such as this one, which occurred on August 10, 1942, on Dyckman Hill Road in Englewood Cliffs.

Bathing:

The Alpine bathing area was closed for bathing for the duration, because of river pollution caused by war conditions. It was operated as a picnic and sun-bathing area, with outdoor showers available for the children and the usual bathhouse and comfort station facilities open for public use.

In view of the discontinuance of bathing, only 50% of the usual number of persons used this area during 1944.

Bloomer's Beach closed after 1941, due to the loss of the Dyckman Street Ferry service, a casualty of wartime gasoline and tire rationing. At Alpine, attendance actually increased, up 33 percent by 1943. This was due, the park speculated, to the fact that the area was easily accessible to a public facing wartime travel restrictions, and the increase reflected "the desire of the public to gain respite from war strains." The following year, the short statement above was placed in the park's *Annual Report*.

Even as beaches and campgrounds closed due to "conditions occasioned by the war," the park remained a popular and ready escape from trying times. Here, on January 16, 1942, barely a month after America's entry into World War II, skaters enjoy Carpenter's Pond atop the Palisades in Fort Lee. A "warming shelter," which can be seen on the right side of the pond, had been built the previous year.

Six

A NEW DEAL FOR THE PALISADES

Shortly after his inauguration in 1933, Franklin Delano Roosevelt set in motion his New Deal for America, which put millions of unemployed men—and teenage boys—to work in federal agencies such as the Civil Works Administration (CWA), the Civilian Conservation Corps (CCC), and the Works Progress Administration (WPA). The park was a beneficiary of the labors of each of these agencies, and much of their work was documented by its photographers.

Together the hundreds of men and boys working for these agencies in the park left a profound legacy expressed in miles of parapet stones and retaining walls along Henry Hudson Drive, in handsome stone picnic tables still in use, in the beautiful Alpine Pavilion (also still in use), and in astounding stone stairways that ascend the Palisades in the most remote and rugged corners of the park.

A more subtle, if no less profound, legacy can be found along the cliff top. Here, in the early 1930s, John D. Rockefeller Jr. took it upon himself to acquire estates and vacant woodlots alike, acting in secret, to provide a gift of hundreds of acres to the interstate commission in 1933. This was done to stave off fears that the new bridge in Fort Lee would bring a spate of development to the summit, marring the commission's initial achievement of preserving this spectacular landscape. Rockefeller placed two stipulations on his gift. First, a "scenic parkway" would be built from the new bridge, across his donated land, and on to Bear Mountain, New York. Second, no man-made structure would be visible from across the river—the Palisades would appear as nature had created them. To the WPA fell the tasks of surveying and laying out the proposed parkway, as well as demolishing the various manor houses and outbuildings—ironically, in its demolition work orders, the agency described these sumptuous dwellings as "undesirable structures"—that had come to seem a permanent part of the cliff edge.

Around 1931, at the start of the worst of the Depression years, work continued on the southern portion of Henry Hudson Drive. The park's workforce was supplemented by laborers sent by the New Jersey Emergency Relief Administration. Groups of 50 men were drawn for daily shifts in Hackensack and provided by the state with transportation and lunch. The park provided hot coffee, cigarettes, and unemployment insurance.

By the time this photograph was taken, on February 5, 1934, Franklin Delano Roosevelt's New Deal policies had been in place almost a year. These men are building a pedestrian underpass beneath Henry Hudson Drive at Lambier Dock in Tenafly. They were among millions of men employed nationwide during the winter months of that year to work for the CWA.

On January 2, 1934, CWA workers stop for a park photographer on Henry Hudson Drive.

Above, on January 12, 1934, a CWA worker hauls stone for the bathhouse and refreshment stand the agency had just begun to build at the Alpine area. By February 5, below, the walls of the Alpine Bathhouse had begun to take shape.

Above, in a photograph also taken on February 5, 1934, the front archway is almost finished, a month after the start of construction. The new buildings were open to the public by Memorial Day 1934. Below is the new bathhouse as it appeared a year later, in July 1935.

In November 1938, a WPA crew works on building bridle paths in the State Line area. (These paths now serve as cross-country ski trails.) The WPA, the largest and most expansive of the New Deal work agencies, would eventually employ millions of men nationwide.

Among the tasks assigned to the WPA in the park was the demolition of many of the large cliff-top estates to make way for the proposed Palisades Interstate Parkway. Above, on October 29, 1935, a crew is razing the manor house at Gray Cliff, the former estate of publisher William Buck Dana in Englewood Cliffs. Below, a crew has begun to remove the roof of the Gray Crag manor house, once the estate of John and Mable Ringling, in Alpine, on November 19 of the same year. (See chapter 3 for photographs of Gray Crag when the Ringlings still lived there.)

On November 7, 1935, a WPA crew lays a foundation for a "comfort station" (restrooms) at the Englewood area, above. Below, on January 13, 1936, a WPA crew works on Henry Hudson Drive.

On February 25, 1936, one group of WPA workers repairs the docks at Englewood Boat Basin, above, while another works on improvements to a locker room in the ferry terminal nearby, below.

On March 4, 1936, above, and on April 28 that same year, below, work proceeds on WPA Project 1-1, improvements on Alpine Approach Road.

Also part of WPA Project 1-1, a crew hauls parapet stones into place at the top of Alpine Approach Road on March 26, 1936.

The photograph above shows the completed CCC camp SP-12, which was built in late 1933 and early 1934 at the park's Greenbrook area on top of the cliffs in Tenafly. A second camp, SP-13, was later built adjacent to SP-12. Below, CCC "boys" (as they were referred to) work on the construction of SP-12 on January 12, 1934. The boys were supposed to be 18 or older, but anecdotal evidence indicates many were younger and lied about their ages to get into the program.

In February 1934, CCC boys work on indoor projects in their newly completed camp buildings. The CCC was more than just a source of employment for the boys, who lived in the camps during their tenure with the program. In addition to room and board, they were paid $30 per month, $25 of which was sent home to their families.

In 1938, CCC boys make repairs to Alpine Approach Road.

In this undated photograph, CCC boys build retaining walls above Henry Hudson Drive, one of the most significant projects the program undertook during its years in the park. These walls still stand.

There was also time for some fun and high jinks during life in the CCC camps. Above, a group of the boys has some fun while plowing Henry Hudson Drive on January 27, 1936. Below is a hand-drawn invitation to a "he-man supper of hot venison" after one of the boys was able to shoot a deer around Christmastime 1940.

This space reserved for Deer

with a little thanks to Varga

Our good time "Hunter" Charlie Weeks
    Bagged a stag and now bespeaks
Your presence and your benison
    At a he-man supper of hot venison.

It may be well to mention here
    You'll find no tempting little
        dears
We would have asked your lady, too
    Had Charlies bag been numbered
        two.

So this offer, we pass on to you
    To turn out - if only to renew
Past friendships that we all
        knew.

Thursday Evening - Dec. 26, 1940
        6:00 P.M.
    C.C.C Camp S.P-12
Englewood   New Jersey

The camps also produced their own small newspapers, which often included pages of comics about camp life such as the one shown here. Other articles focused on health and safety issues, reports about work projects, camp news, and information about upcoming social events such as dances.

On March 13, 1936, CCC boys work to repair damage after a washout along Henry Hudson Drive.

Seven

AN OASIS IN THE MODERN WORLD

The end of World War II saw a park utterly transformed from what it had been only a few years earlier. Its infrastructure was still in place, but its bathing beaches and campgrounds were closed. Likewise, some profound changes were taking hold of the region. After a decade and a half of economic depression and war, the effects of the George Washington Bridge and the age of the automobile were finally making themselves felt beyond the park. Modern suburbs were beginning to flourish in northeastern New Jersey. On the Palisades, John D. Rockefeller Jr.'s dream of a parkway along the cliff top began to become a reality. (A nature sanctuary was born there as well.)

Along the riverfront, areas such as Forest View, with its ball field and picnic groves—but not a single accommodation for automobiles—would be abandoned. Other picnic areas would continue to thrive, although visitors came by car now rather than ferry or excursion boat. Two boat basins continued to operate in the park, their slips filled to capacity during the boating season. Hiking also remained popular (the two main trails in the park, the Long Path and the Hudson River Shore Trail, would be designated national historic and recreation trails, and the Palisades themselves a national natural landmark).

All this remains true today, and several new demographics have entered into the park in recent decades as well. Most notable are cyclists, for whom Henry Hudson Drive has become a haven in the metropolitan area. In recent years, there has been a resurgence of paddlers, although the preferred craft these days is the kayak rather than the canoe.

Faced with these changes, the park itself has changed, with more emphasis on educational programs and the like, the development of facilities such as Fort Lee Historic Park, and a new "living history" approach to programming at the historic Kearney House.

What has not changed, of course, is the scenic beauty preserved over a century ago, a legacy left to all, and for all who follow.

In 1938, what remains today the largest rock slide in the park's history occurred about a mile north of the Alpine area, shown in the photograph above. Several years later, in 1941, this rock slide took on a strange life of its own, as people across the river in Yonkers began to claim that a face could be seen in the cliffs where the slide occurred, as shown in the photograph below. It was not just any face they saw but one of a man very much in the news at the time: Adolf Hitler. (The "face" can be seen in the left-hand side of the light-colored portion of the cliffs immediately above the pile of fallen rock.) The story made it to the national wire services as well as the local press (a headline from the *Northern Valley Tribune* on April 18, 1941, read, "Hitler Haunts the Hudson in Stone as Cold as His Heart"). The story took an even more eerie turn in 1945 when, just months after Hitler's defeat, another rock slide wiped the unwelcome face off the mountainside forever.

By the early 20th century, it was widely believed that the Hudson River had been "fished out." But with the advent of the Great Depression, unemployed men along the river, figuring they had little to lose by trying, began to set nets for the springtime shad run again. To their surprise, the catches were large, and by the mid-1930s, the park had to issue permits by lottery for shad fishing along its shore. The newly reopened fisheries continued to flourish for years, as shown by these photographs taken in Alpine in May 1945.

With the end of World War II, the park commission resumed its plans to construct a scenic parkway along the cliff top. An early sketch of the proposed roadway is shown above. Below, in 1945, a governor's inspection tour—which included John D. Rockefeller Jr., third from left—has come to the park to inspect the proposed route of the new highway (the tour included a stop at Alpine Boat Basin).

Partly as a result of public concern that the new parkway would detract from the scenic beauty and tranquility of the Palisades cliff top, a nature sanctuary was proposed for the Greenbrook area in Tenafly and Alpine. Greenbrook Sanctuary, managed by the Palisades Nature Association, was established in 1946. In October 1948, the Garden Club of New Jersey dedicated an arboretum in the new 165-acre sanctuary. Pictured are Mrs. Laurence Wilson and Mrs. Herman Cook.

A page from the park commission's *Annual Report* for 1955, reporting on the dedication of the Rockefeller Lookout along the new parkway in Englewood Cliffs, is shown above. The ceremony was held in May of that year, although it would still be several years before the entire parkway up to Bear Mountain, New York, would be completed. Pictured from left to right are park commissioners Theodore Boettger, Catesby L. Jones, Horace M. Albright, Albert R. Jube, George W. Perkins, Donald G. Borg, and Laurance S. Rockefeller, and general manager A. K. Morgan.

On January 8, 1948, park patrolman Jim Sacco tries doing his rounds on snowshoes, with the George Washington Bridge in the background. (Although it makes for a pretty picture, the experiment of placing officers on snowshoes proved infelicitous.)

Even as the park's beaches and campgrounds continued to close with the onset of World War II, it remained a popular destination for those seeking a quick escape into the country, as shown in this photograph taken near the park's Englewood Cliffs entrance around that time.

Closed during the war years, State Line Lookout's Lookout Inn reopened after the war, as shown in these photographs from late-summer 1949. As work commenced on the parkway, an entrance to the State Line Lookout area was incorporated into the new highway using the former path of U.S. Route 9W.

Although it no longer offered camping facilities after the war, Ross Dock continued to be popular with picnickers (and remains so to this day), such as this group in 1949.

Like many others, Helen Soka (left) and her friend Jean Staffon would sometimes take a trolley from their homes in New York City to Yonkers and then take the Yonkers Ferry across the river to the park for a day of exploration. Here they are pictured around 1945 near Forest View, with the Indian Head profile visible in the cliff face behind them. (Courtesy of Helen Soka.)

Students from Columbia University take in the view from Fort Lee during a geology field trip in November 1949. Students at the university continue to make such excursions to this day.

By 1949, the venerable Dyckman Street Ferry had finally ceased operation, as shown by this photograph of the desolate pilings of its former dock in the park in that year.

Opened in 1976 to coincide with the commemoration of the nation's bicentennial, the park's 33-acre Fort Lee Historic Park on the cliff top provides a unique "living history" program for schoolchildren, who can spend a day as "recruits" in the Continental army. The historic park also hosts Revolutionary War reenactments, during which an 18th-century mortar may be fired—with the George Washington Bridge and upper Manhattan as the backdrop.

In 2001, during the 225th anniversary of the events of November 1776, British "soldiers" once again ascend the old Huyler's Landing Road (now a hiking trail) to reenact the invasion of New Jersey.

122

The Kearney House returns to being a 19th-century riverfront tavern several evenings each fall and spring, in a program called Punch and Pie at Mrs. Kearney's Tavern. Shown mingling with 21st-century guests during such an evening are Kearney House director Eric Nelsen (standing) and Fort Lee Historic Park director John Muller.

The Hudson River sloop *Clearwater*, a reproduction of a typical 19th-century vessel, launched in 1969 through the efforts of, among others, the folksinger Pete Seeger, sails past Alpine Boat Basin, one of its regular ports of call. The sloop takes school groups and others out for educational sails on the river.

Henry Herbert Oltman's Penlyn is the last survivor of the majestic estates that once dotted the cliff top, today serving as the park's headquarters building (and a rest stop for cyclists and other park visitors), above. Other manor houses, such as George Zabriskie's Cliff Dale, below, remain as evocative ruins discovered by hikers along the trails.

The park serves as an oasis in the modern metropolis 12 months a year. At right, a youngster enjoys a snowy day at Point Lookout at State Line Lookout. Below, a camera pointed north toward Bombay Hook from the Alpine area captures a moment of early-morning tranquility in the late summer.

The park continues to expand its public programs, such as hikes for children and other activities. Above, a mother and her son stop along the shore during one of these programs in 2006.

In 2004, the park hosted a rededication ceremony for the 75th anniversary of the cliff-top "watchtower" monument that had been erected in Alpine in 1929 to honor the role of the New Jersey State Federation of Women's Clubs in preserving the Palisades.

The bathhouse built at Alpine by the CWA in 1934 (see chapter 6) remains an important facility for the park and its visitors, now used as a picnic pavilion for activities ranging from weddings and family get-togethers to folk dances and celebrations.

In recent years, peregrine falcons, once driven to the brink of extinction by pesticide pollution, have come back to the ledges of the Palisades—the tall cliffs of the Hudson River may be the first place in New Jersey where these magnificent animals have returned to their former natural nest sites. (Photograph by Nancy Slowik.)

Across America, People are Discovering Something Wonderful. Their Heritage.

Arcadia Publishing is the leading local history publisher in the United States. With more than 3,000 titles in print and hundreds of new titles released every year, Arcadia has extensive specialized experience chronicling the history of communities and celebrating America's hidden stories, bringing to life the people, places, and events from the past. To discover the history of other communities across the nation, please visit:

www.arcadiapublishing.com

Customized search tools allow you to find regional history books about the town where you grew up, the cities where your friends and family live, the town where your parents met, or even that retirement spot you've been dreaming about.